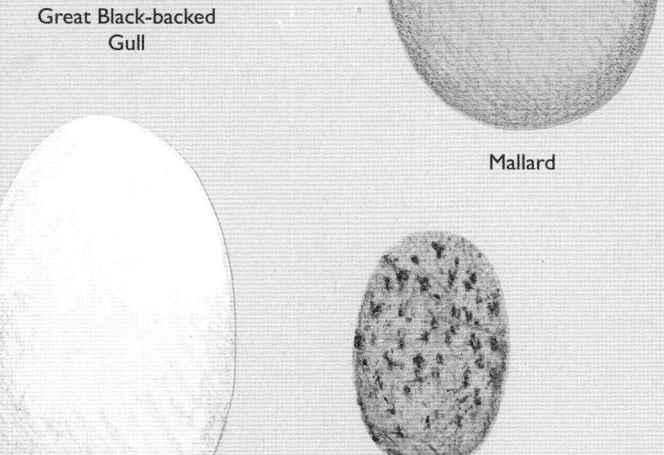
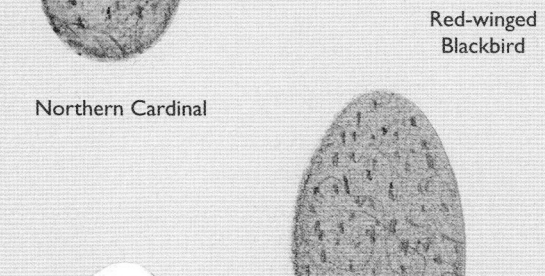

Arctic Tern

Barn Swallow

Rufous
Hummingbird

Mourning Warbler

Red Crossbill

Black-throated
Blue Warbler

Great Black-backed
Gull

Blue Jay

Black-and-white
Warbler

Mallard

Black-billed Magpie

Red-winged
Blackbird

Double-crested
Cormorant

Northern Cardinal

American Robin

Snowy Owl

Steller's Jay

Yellow-headed
Blackbird

Scarlet Tanager

Mourning Dove

Golden Eagle

Ruby-throated
Hummingbird

Yellow Warbler

Tufted Puffin

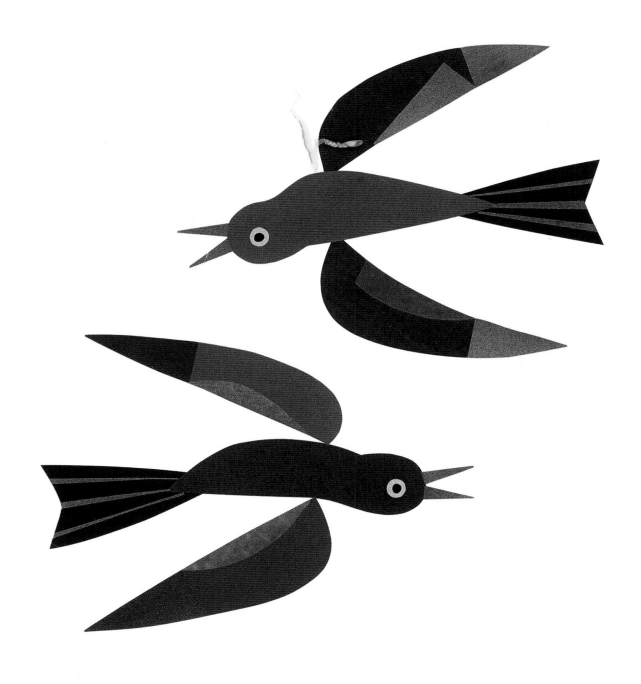

For Craig, with love

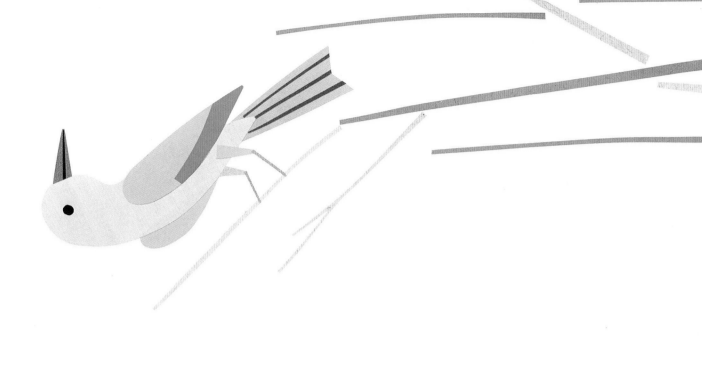

Groundwood Books / House of Anansi Press
110 Spadina Avenue, Suite 801, Toronto, Ontario M5V 2K4
or c/o Publishers Group West
1700 Fourth Street, Berkeley, CA 94710

We acknowledge for their financial support of our publishing
program the Canada Council for the Arts, the Ontario Arts
Council and the Government of Canada.

Canada Council   Conseil des Arts
for the Arts   du Canada

ONTARIO ARTS COUNCIL
CONSEIL DES ARTS DE L'ONTARIO
an Ontario government agency
un organisme du gouvernement de l'Ontario

With the participation of the Government of Canada
Avec la participation du gouvernement du Canada   Canadä

Library and Archives Canada Cataloguing in Publication
Valério, Geraldo, author
My book of birds / Geraldo Valério.
Issued in print and electronic formats.
ISBN 978-1-55498-800-6 (bound). —
ISBN 978-1-55498-801-3 (pdf)
1. Birds — Juvenile literature. 2. Birds — Pictorial works —
Juvenile literature. I. Title.
QL676.2.V35 2016   j598   C2015-903594-5
C2015-903595-3

The illustrations were created with old magazine paper, art
paper, gift wrap, scissors and glue, with color pencil and
gouache for the endpapers. The eggs and feathers on the
endpapers are not to scale.
Design by Michael Solomon
Edited by Nan Froman
Printed and bound in Malaysia

MIX
Paper from
responsible sources
FSC FSC® C012700
www.fsc.org

GROUNDWOOD BOOKS   HOUSE OF ANANSI PRESS   TORONTO   BERKELEY

GERALDO VALÉRIO

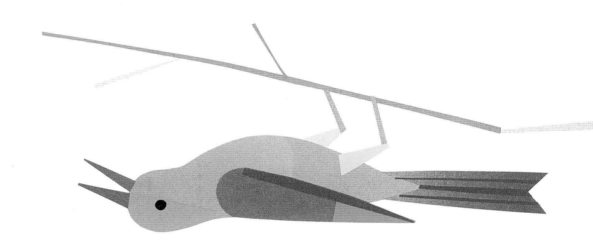

MY BOOK of BIRDS

INTRODUCTION

GROWING UP IN BRAZIL, I spent a lot of time playing with my friends along the shore of the river that ran close to my house. I saw families of white egrets and noisy parakeets. I watched wild Muscovy Ducks swimming with their little chicks. Up above me, I would see Black Vultures and flocks of swallows that looked like moving clouds.

I love the variety of birds, their colored feathers and their sense of freedom.

When I moved to Canada, I discovered many birds new to me. For the first time I saw cormorants, sandpipers, gulls, jays and warblers. Herons, too!

I have always been fascinated by books about birds, including the wondrous pictures of John James Audubon. For years now, I have been making collages of birds using old magazine paper. Collage allows me to capture the sense of aliveness and joy I feel when I look at birds. The image is a door that leads me to discover and learn.

My Book of Birds is my album of artistic impressions of North American birds. Learning about these birds makes me happy, and I hope *My Book of Birds* will make you happy, too.

In parts of Asia, Golden Eagles are still trained as hunting birds in the ancient art of falconry.

6

Golden Eagle
Aquila chrysaetos

The Golden Eagle is an awesome bird of prey. It flies over fields and mountains searching for animals like rabbits, hares and marmots. Then it dives at high speed, grasping its prey with sharp talons.

American White Pelican
Pelecanus erythrorhynchos

American White Pelicans are very social birds. When it is time to feed, they often team up to catch fish. The pelicans beat their wings and poke their large bills into the water to steer a school of fish to shore. Then they gobble them up.

Osprey
Pandion haliaetus

Ospreys mostly eat fish, and they are very good at catching them. They fly high above lakes and rivers until they spot a fish, then suddenly drop to the water with their talons stretched out in front of them.

Ospreys can wrap their talons around both sides of a fish for a tight grip. Spiky areas on the underside of their toes also help them hold onto their catch.

Swallows are small birds with long pointy wings. They are smooth and speedy flyers and can easily catch insects in the air.

Swallows probably first came from Africa, but now they can be found almost all over the world. Many species migrate to warm climates for the winter.

Purple Martin
Progne subis

Purple Martins are the biggest swallows in North America. Many are fond of nesting in houses where they can live next door to their friends!

Violet-green Swallow
Tachycineta thalassina

These colorful western swallows sometimes flock together to chase flying insects.

Barn Swallow
Hirundo rustica

Like most swallows, Barn Swallows swoop down to sip water from ponds, lakes and rivers while in flight.

Snowy Owl
Bubo scandiacus

These huge owls nest on the Arctic tundra. In years when there is plenty of prey, especially lemmings, they may lay up to a dozen eggs. The baby owls have soft white feathers when they hatch, but they soon turn a blackish-gray. Both parents look after their young and bravely drive away Arctic foxes, wolves, ravens and other predators.

Snowy Owls hunt both day and night. Like many birds, they gulp down their prey whole and later spit up pellets of its fur or feathers, bones and teeth.

15

Hummingbirds are some of the smallest birds in the world. They flap their wings so quickly that they seem to float in the air as they dip their bills into flowers to drink nectar. They also eat little insects, often in flight.

These tiny birds can fly at high speeds, and they can even fly upside down and backwards!

Rufous Hummingbird
Selasphorus rufus

The female Rufous Hummingbird builds a very small nest from plants and spider webs, then hides it with lichens. She lays two tiny, tiny eggs inside.

Ruby-throated Hummingbird
Archilochus colubris

Look for Ruby-throated Hummingbirds in the gardens and woods of the east. In the fall they fly south, sometimes as far as Costa Rica or Panama.

Pileated Woodpecker
Dryocopus pileatus

This very large woodpecker with a bright red crest noisily drums away on logs and dead trees in search of its favorite meal — carpenter ants.

    The male and female also chip away on dead wood to make a large hole for their nest. Once they have left, the hole may be occupied by other creatures such as bats, owls or even raccoons.

Northern Flicker
Colaptes auratus

The Northern Flicker drills into the soil to find ants and their larvae, which it captures with its long tongue.

When these woodpeckers fly, you can often see a lovely color underneath their wings and tails. Yellow-shafted flickers are usually found in the east; red-shafted flickers in the west.

Black-capped Chickadee
Poecile atricapillus

This sweet little bird is lively and curious. It spends most of its time searching for food and helps us by eating insects that damage farm crops. It also eats spiders, berries and seeds, and it likes to hide seeds away for a future feast.

Marsh Wren
Cistothorus palustris

You can identify a wren by its upturned tail.
At breeding time the male Marsh Wren never
seems to stop singing. He begins to weave a
number of cocoon-shaped nests in the reeds,
since he may have more than one mate. A female
chooses a nest and places fine grass inside.

Common Raven
Corvus corax

Ravens are huge, dramatic-looking birds with a deep croak, found most often in the wild but sometimes in towns and cities, too. They are skilled and daring in flight. They are also very smart. Two ravens sometimes help one another catch prey, and if they have more food than they can eat, they store some away. Ravens eat everything from other birds' eggs to small mammals, frogs, insects, carrion — even garbage.

American Crow
Corvus brachyrhynchos

American Crows are smaller and more social than ravens. They often live in flocks, and in the winter thousands gather in trees to roost for the night. Crow families stay together for a long time, with young birds helping to raise the new hatchlings.

Crows are also clever, especially where food is concerned! They sometimes follow other birds to their nests, where they return later to eat the eggs or young. They drop clam or mussel shells onto hard rocks to open them.

Tanagers return to their tropical homes in the winter — Scarlet Tanagers to South America and Western Tanagers to Mexico and Central America. They often wait until nightfall to make their southward journey.

Scarlet Tanager
Piranga olivacea

If you are lucky on a summer day, you might spot the bright male Scarlet Tanager high in an eastern treetop. In the fall his red feathers molt to a greeny-yellow, making him look more like the female.

Western Tanager
Piranga ludoviciana

Western Tanagers eat many insects, including dragonflies. But first they snip off the dragonfly's wings!

Rose-breasted Grosbeak
Pheucticus ludovicianus

Rose-breasted Grosbeaks sing sweetly, especially when the male comes to sit on the nest.

Northern Cardinal
Cardinalis cardinalis

The female cardinal's soft colors are a pleasant contrast to the male's bright red.
Unlike their grosbeak cousins, cardinals do not migrate to a warmer climate in the winter.

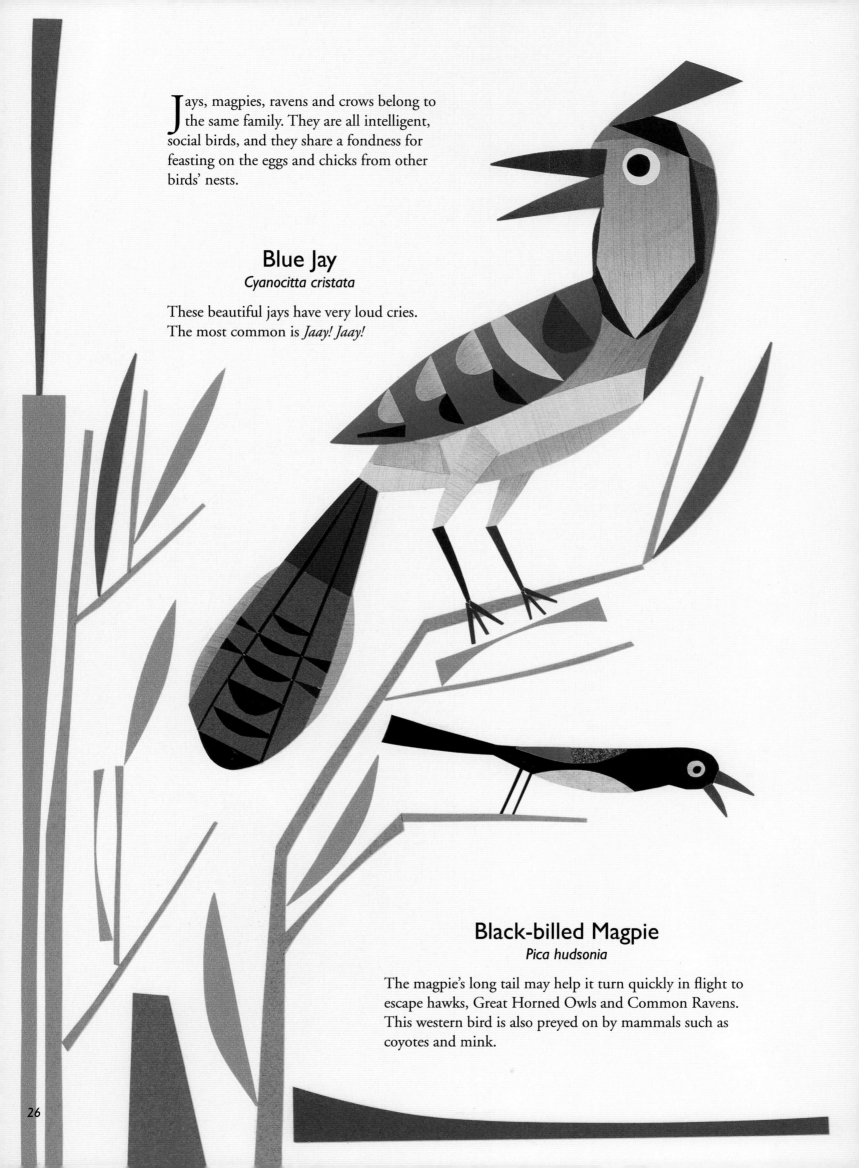

Jays, magpies, ravens and crows belong to the same family. They are all intelligent, social birds, and they share a fondness for feasting on the eggs and chicks from other birds' nests.

Blue Jay
Cyanocitta cristata

These beautiful jays have very loud cries. The most common is *Jaay! Jaay!*

Black-billed Magpie
Pica hudsonia

The magpie's long tail may help it turn quickly in flight to escape hawks, Great Horned Owls and Common Ravens. This western bird is also preyed on by mammals such as coyotes and mink.

Steller's Jay
Cyanocitta stelleri

The daring Steller's Jay, found in the west, is very good at imitating the sounds of other birds, and even dogs and cats.

Trumpeter Swan
Cygnus buccinator

These huge swans — the biggest in the world — were almost extinct a hundred years ago because they were so widely prized for their feathers, eggs and skin. Thanks to the work of conservationists, Trumpeter Swans are increasing in number, although humans now threaten the freshwater lakes, marshes and rivers where they live.

A young swan is called a cygnet.

A female swan sits on a nest of plants near the water.

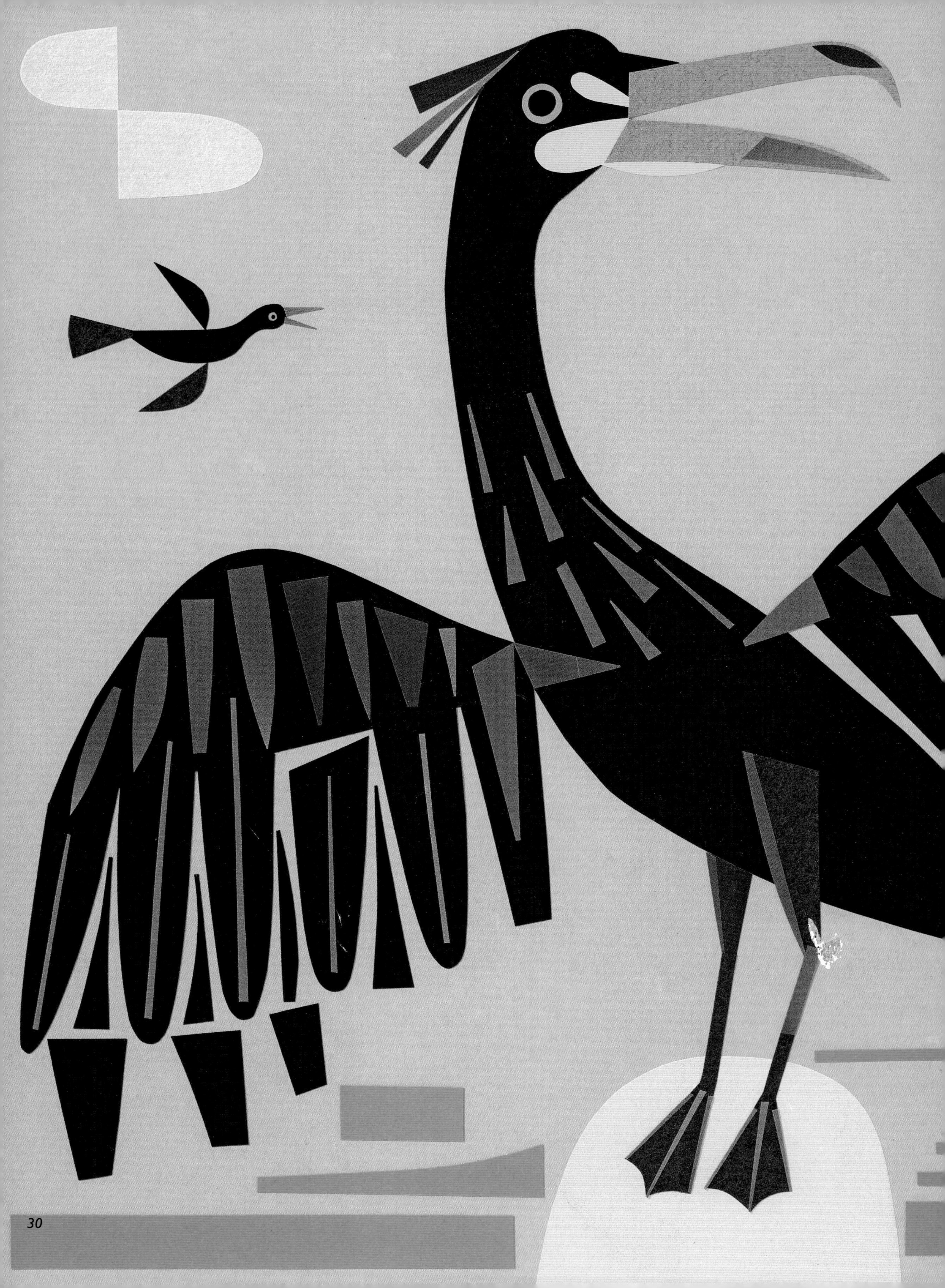

Double-crested Cormorant
Phalacrocorax auritus

Cormorants gather in large numbers near oceans and lakes, where they dive for fish. Afterward they like to find a place to dry their glossy black wings.

These striking birds are named for the feathery crests that appear on their heads at breeding time.

The cormorant's webbed feet help it swim swiftly underwater.

Great Blue Heron
Ardea herodias

This elegant bird lives in swamps and marshes, and along the shores of lakes, rivers and oceans. It walks calmly through shallow water searching for food, then suddenly snatches up little fish with its bill.

Herons breed in small, noisy colonies. They often build their large nests up in trees to protect the eggs and young from predators.

Great Black-backed Gull
Larus marinus

If you visit a beach along the North Atlantic coast, you will probably see these gulls — the biggest in the world — diving to catch fish or scavenging for picnic leftovers.

Great Black-backed Gulls are very pushy. They are known for stealing from other birds — not only food, but their eggs and young as well!

Arctic Tern
Sterna paradisaea

Arctic Terns migrate farther than any other bird. Every year they
fly all the way from the Arctic, where they nest, to Antarctica
and back. It's not surprising that they spend most of their time in
flight, usually far out at sea.

Mallard

Anas platyrhynchos

You can see these ducks in the city and country, near fresh water and salt water, especially if the water is not too deep and there are lots of plants to eat. The brightly colored male is easy to spot. The female makes the familiar quack — a flock of Mallards can be very loud!

The female may lay as many as fifteen eggs in a nest on the ground, usually hidden from lurking predators. Shortly after the fluffy ducklings emerge from the shell, she takes them for a swim.

Whooping Crane
Grus americana

Whooping Cranes do a special dance when they choose their mates. These tall, graceful cranes were once almost extinct because of hunting and loss of habitat, and they are still endangered. But conservation groups are working hard to ensure their survival.